GROWTH STRATEGIES FOR INTERNATIONAL BUSINESS DEVELOPMENT

DR. JAGADEESH PILLAI

Made with ❤ on the Notion Press Platform
www.notionpress.com

|| Dedicated to all wisdom seekers around the world ||

༃

Contents

Contents

PRAYER

**"Om Bhadram Karnebhih Shrunuyaama
DevaahBhadram Pashyemaakshabhiryajatraah
SthirairangaistushtuvaamsastanoobhihVyashema
Devahitam YadaayuhSwasti Na Indro
VridhashravaahSwasti Nah Pooshaa
VishwavedaahSwasti Nastaarkshyo ArishtanemihSwasti
No Brihaspatir DadhaatuOm Shantih, Shantih, Shantih"**

The literal meaning of this mantra is: OM. O Gods! Let us
hear auspicious words from our ears. O reverent Gods! Let
us behold propitious visions from our eyes, let our organs
and body be stable, healthy, and strong. Let us do that
which is pleasing to the gods in the life span allotted to us.
May Indra, inscribed in the scriptures, bring us fortune!
May Pushan, the knower of the world, grant us prosperity!
May Trakshya, who vanquishes enemies, bestow us with
blessings! May Brihaspati bring us success!
OM Peace, Peace, Peace.

About The Author

Dr. Jagadeesh Pillai is a renowned Guinness World Record holder, writer, and researcher hailing from Varanasi, also known as the abode of Lord Shiva. With a Ph.D. in Vedic Science and a range of creative ideas and achievements, he is a true polymath. He is the author of more than 100 books including Research Publications. Although his roots can be traced back to Kerala, the people of Varanasi hold him in high regard and affectionately consider him one of their own.

In 1998, Dr. Pillai was offered a job at Banaras Hindu University, but he left the position after only two months to pursue greater goals in life. He believed that in order to study Indian scriptures and engage in other creative endeavours, he needed to retire from the daily grind of working solely for money at a young age.

He started an export business from scratch, using the knowledge he had gained from a previous job in the industry. His intelligence and unique approach to business led to great success in a short period of time, earning him more in just a decade and a half than he would have in a lifetime working in a government job. Upon the passing of Dr. APJ Abdul Kalam, Dr. Pillai decided to leave the business and dedicate himself to reading, studying, researching, and experimenting.

During his tenure in the export business, Dr. Pillai traveled to over 16 countries, gaining valuable insight and experiencing the world and life in detail.

Dr. Pillai has achieved four Guinness World Records in the following subjects:

"Script to Screen" - In this record, Dr. Pillai produced and directed an animation film within the shortest time possible, breaking the previous record set by Canadians. He has also received numerous national and international awards and recognitions for this achievement.

Longest Line of Postcards - For this record, Dr. Pillai created a line of 16,300 postcards on the occasion of the 163rd anniversary of Indian Postal Day. The event also included a questionnaire about the Indian flag.

Largest Poster Awareness Campaign - Dr. Pillai designed an awareness campaign on the subject of "Beti Bachao - Beti Padhao" (Save the Girl Child - Educate the Girl Child) to achieve this record.

Largest Envelope - In tribute to the Indian Prime Minister's "Make in India" initiative, Dr. Pillai created a 4000 square meter envelope using waste paper to achieve this record.

Attempted - **70000 Candles on a 210 kg Cake** - To celebrate the 70th Indian Independence Day, Dr. Pillai attempted to light 70,000 candles on a 210 kg cake, which was recorded in World Records India.

Attempted - **Documentary on Dhamek Stupa of Sarnath in 17 Languages** - Dr. Pillai attempted to create a documentary on the Dhamek Stupa of Sarnath, dubbing it in 17 different languages. The result of this attempt is currently awaiting confirmation from the Guinness World Records.

Dr. Pillai is skilled in teaching the Bhagavad Gita, a Hindu scripture, and is popular among young people. He has helped many young people improve their lives through his motivational teachings.

In addition to teaching, he has composed and sung numerous Sanskrit Bhajans and patriotic songs.

He has also written and directed several short films and documentaries for awareness campaigns, and has volunteered with the police in both UP and Kerala to spread awareness about various issues through videos and photography.

Incredibly, he has produced and directed over 100 documentaries about the city of Varanasi, all on his own.

He has also helped and guided more than 25 boys and girls to achieve world records through creative and innovative methods. He is a multifaceted person who uses his intellect and the blessings given to him by God to excel in various areas. He is both a teacher and a student, always learning and teaching, and is able to master any subject he comes across.

He is a selfless social activist and motivational speaker who has overcome struggles and failures to become a successful and enthusiastic individual with a rich life experience.

In addition to his work with the Bhagavad Gita, he is also an efficient Tarot card reader, Astro-Vastu consultant, and a talented singer and composer. He has sung the entire Ram Charita Manas and Bhagavad Gita in his own compositions, and has sung the phrase "Lokah Samastha Sukhino Bhavantu" in 50 different languages. He is currently working on a detailed and scientific study of Vedas, Upanishads, Puranas, and the Bhagavad Gita. He has also composed and sung the Hanuman Chalisa and Gayatri Mantra in 108 and 1008 different compositions, respectively.

Awards - Four Times Guinness World Records, Winner of Mahatma Gandhi Vishwa Shanti Puraskar, Mahatma Gandhi Global Peace Ambassador, Kashi Ratna Award, Dr. APJ Abdul Kalam Motivational Person of the Year 2017, Mother Teresa Award, Indira Gandhi Priyadarshini Award, Bharat Vikas Ratna Award, Udyog Ratna Award, Vigyan Prasar Award, Poorvanchal Ratn Samman.

PREFACE

As the world continues to become increasingly interconnected, the need for global growth strategies for international business development has never been greater. With the rise of digital technology, the ability to reach customers and markets around the world has become easier than ever before. However, the challenge of navigating the complexities of international business development remains.

This book, "Global Growth Strategies for International Business Development", provides a comprehensive guide to the strategies and tactics necessary for successful international business development. It covers topics such as market entry strategies, cultural considerations, and legal and regulatory frameworks. It also provides practical advice on how to develop and implement effective global growth strategies.

This book is an invaluable resource for anyone looking to expand their business into international markets. It is written in an accessible and engaging style, making it easy to understand and apply the strategies and tactics discussed. Whether you are a business owner, a manager, or an entrepreneur, this book will provide you with the knowledge and tools you need to succeed in the global marketplace.

This book is a must-read for anyone looking to expand their business into international markets. It provides a comprehensive guide to the strategies and tactics necessary for successful international business development, and offers practical advice on how to develop and implement effective global growth strategies. With its accessible and engaging style, this book is an invaluable resource for anyone looking to take their business to the next level.

I

Introduction to International Business Development

International business development is a process of identifying and pursuing opportunities for growth and expansion in foreign markets. It is an essential component of a company's overall strategy for achieving global success. The chapter will provide an overview of the key concepts, challenges, and opportunities of international business development.

The first step in international business development is to conduct a thorough market analysis to identify potential target markets. This includes assessing the economic, political, and cultural environment of the target market, as well as understanding the needs and preferences of the target customers. Once a target market has been identified, companies must then develop a strategy for entering the market. This may involve exporting goods or services, establishing a joint venture with a local partner, or setting up a wholly-owned subsidiary.

One of the major challenges of international business development is managing the risks associated with doing business in foreign markets. This includes political risks such as changes in government policies or instability, as well as economic risks such as currency fluctuations or changes in trade regulations. Companies must also be aware of cultural differences and tailor their products and services to meet the needs of the target market.

In addition to these challenges, international business development also presents a number of opportunities for companies. For example, entering new markets can provide access to new customers and potential sources of revenue. It can also help to diversify a company's product or service offerings and increase overall competitiveness.

In conclusion, international business development is a critical component of achieving global success for companies. It requires a thorough understanding of target markets and the ability to navigate the challenges and opportunities presented by doing business in foreign markets. The chapter provides an overview of the key concepts and challenges of international business development, as well as highlighting the opportunities for growth and expansion in foreign markets.

II

Globalization and the International Business Environment

Globalization is the process by which businesses and other organizations develop international influence or start operating on an international scale. It is a result of advances in technology, transportation, and communication that have made it easier and more efficient to conduct business across borders. As a result, companies are increasingly operating in a global business environment.

The international business environment is made up of a complex web of economic, political, cultural, and legal factors that can affect a company's ability to operate in foreign markets. Economic factors include exchange rates, inflation, and economic growth. Political factors include government stability, trade policies, and regulations. Cultural factors include differences in language, customs, and consumer preferences. Legal factors include the protection of intellectual property and compliance with international trade agreements.

Globalization has led to increased competition among companies as they compete for customers and resources in foreign markets. As a result, companies must be able to adapt to different business environments and be able to navigate the challenges and opportunities presented by the global economy.

One of the key challenges of globalization is managing cultural differences. Companies must be able to understand and respect the cultural norms of the countries in which they operate. This includes understanding local laws and customs, as well as being able to effectively communicate with customers and business partners.

Another challenge is the need to comply with different legal and regulatory requirements in each country. Companies must be aware of the laws and regulations that apply to their operations in foreign markets, and ensure that they are in compliance with them.

Despite these challenges, globalization presents a number of opportunities for companies. For example, it allows companies to access new customers and potential sources of revenue. It also allows companies to access new resources and technologies.

In conclusion, the international business environment is complex and constantly changing. Globalization has led to increased competition among companies, and companies must be able to navigate the challenges and opportunities presented by the global economy in order to be successful. The chapter provides an overview of globalization and the international business environment, highlighting the key challenges and opportunities that companies face in the global market.

III

Cultural Intelligence and Cross-cultural Management

Cultural intelligence, also known as cultural quotient (CQ), is the ability to understand, appreciate, and effectively navigate cultural differences. It is becoming increasingly important in today's global business environment as companies operate in more diverse and multicultural markets.

Cross-cultural management is the process of managing and leading people from different cultural backgrounds. This includes understanding how culture influences communication, decision-making, and behavior, and being able to adapt management styles and strategies to be effective in different cultural contexts.

Cultural intelligence can be developed through a combination of cognitive, physical, and emotional skills. Cognitive skills include knowledge and understanding of different cultures, as well as the ability to think critically and make decisions in cross-cultural contexts. Physical skills include the ability to navigate unfamiliar environments and adapt to different social norms. Emotional skills include the ability to manage emotions and maintain positive relationships with people from different cultural backgrounds.

Effective cross-cultural management requires the ability to understand and appreciate cultural differences, as well as the ability to adapt management styles and strategies to be effective in different cultural contexts. This includes being able to effectively communicate with people from different cultures, as well as being able to navigate cultural differences in decision-making, negotiation, and conflict resolution.

One important aspect of cross-cultural management is being able to understand and appreciate cultural differences in communication styles. This includes understanding the role of nonverbal communication, such as facial expressions and body language, as well as being able to effectively communicate in different languages.

Another important aspect is being able to understand and appreciate cultural differences in decision-making styles. This includes understanding how different cultures approach risk-taking, negotiation, and problem-solving.

In conclusion, cultural intelligence and cross-cultural management are becoming increasingly important in today's global business environment. Effective cross-cultural management requires the ability to understand, appreciate, and effectively navigate cultural differences, as well as the ability to adapt management styles and strategies to be effective in different cultural contexts. The chapter provides an overview of cultural intelligence and cross-cultural management, highlighting the key skills and strategies needed to be successful in a global business environment.

IV

International Market Research and Analysis

International market research and analysis is the process of gathering and analyzing information about potential international markets to identify opportunities and risks. This information can be used to inform strategic business decisions, such as where to expand operations, what products or services to offer, and how to price and market them.

There are several steps involved in conducting international market research and analysis. The first step is to define the research objectives, which should be specific, measurable, and achievable. The next step is to identify the target market, which should be defined in terms of geographic, demographic, and psychographic characteristics.

Once the target market has been identified, the next step is to collect data. This can be done through a variety of methods, including surveys, interviews, focus groups, and secondary research. The data collected should be analyzed to identify trends, patterns, and insights that can inform business decisions.

One important aspect of international market research and analysis is understanding cultural differences. Different cultures can have different needs, wants, and expectations, and it's important to take this into account when conducting research and analyzing data. For example, a product that is successful in one country may not be successful in another country because of cultural differences in taste or preferences.

Another important aspect of international market research and analysis is understanding the competitive landscape. This includes identifying the key competitors, understanding their strengths and weaknesses, and understanding the competitive dynamics of the market.

In conclusion, international market research and analysis is an essential process for any company that is considering expanding into international markets. It provides valuable information that can inform strategic business decisions and help companies to identify opportunities and mitigate risks. The chapter provides an overview of the process of international market research and analysis, highlighting the key steps, methods, and considerations involved in conducting research and analyzing data in a global business environment.

DR. JAGADEESH PILLAI

V

International Marketing and Branding

Marketing and branding are essential components of any international business strategy. They help companies to create a positive image, build customer loyalty, and increase sales in new markets.

When it comes to international marketing, it's important to understand that different cultures can have different preferences and buying habits. Therefore, it's crucial to tailor marketing strategies to the specific market. This includes adapting product packaging, advertising messages, and pricing strategies to suit the local culture.

One of the key elements of international marketing is market segmentation. This involves dividing the market into smaller groups of customers with similar needs, wants, and behaviors. By understanding these groups, companies can develop targeted marketing campaigns that are more likely to resonate with the target audience.

Another important aspect of international marketing is understanding the distribution channels. Different countries have different distribution systems, and it's important to be aware of these when entering a new market. For example, in some countries, it's common to sell products through retail outlets, while in others, it's more common to sell through distributors or agents.

Branding is another important aspect of international marketing. A strong brand can help to build customer loyalty, increase sales, and create a positive image in new markets. However, it's important to be aware that different cultures can have different perceptions of brands. Therefore, it's crucial to tailor branding strategies to the specific market.

In conclusion, international marketing and branding are essential components of any international business strategy. They help companies to create a positive image, build customer loyalty, and increase sales in new markets. However, it's important to understand that different cultures can have different preferences and buying habits. Therefore, it's crucial to tailor marketing and branding strategies to the specific market. This chapter provides an overview of the key elements of international marketing and branding, highlighting the importance of understanding cultural differences, market segmentation, distribution channels and the importance of strong branding.

GLOBAL GROWTH STRATEGIES FOR INTERNATIONAL BUSINESS DEVELOPMENT

VI

International Sales and Distribution

International sales and distribution are critical components of any international business strategy. They help companies to reach new customers, increase revenue, and expand into new markets. However, there are a number of challenges that companies need to be aware of when it comes to international sales and distribution.

One of the key challenges is understanding the different regulations and laws that apply in different countries. These can include import and export regulations, tariffs, and taxes. It's important for companies to be aware of these regulations and to ensure that they comply with them. Failure to do so can result in fines, penalties, and even criminal charges.

Another challenge is understanding the different distribution channels that are used in different countries.

In some countries, it's common to sell products through retail outlets, while in others, it's more common to sell through distributors or agents. It's important for companies to be aware of these distribution channels and to choose the most appropriate one for their products.

Another important aspect of international sales and distribution is pricing. Prices can vary greatly from country to country, and it's important for companies to be aware of these differences. In some countries, prices may be higher due to higher labor or material costs, while in others, prices may be lower due to lower taxes or other factors.

In conclusion, international sales and distribution are critical components of any international business strategy. They help companies to reach new customers, increase revenue, and expand into new markets. However, there are a number of challenges that companies need to be aware of when it comes to international sales and distribution. These include understanding the different regulations and laws that apply in different countries, understanding the different distribution channels that are used in different countries, and understanding the different prices that are used in different countries. This chapter provides an overview of the key elements of international sales and distribution, highlighting the importance of compliance with laws, understanding distribution channels and pricing strategies in different countries.

VII

International Pricing and Promotion

International pricing and promotion are important elements of any international business strategy. They help companies to reach new customers, increase revenue, and expand into new markets. However, there are a number of challenges that companies need to be aware of when it comes to international pricing and promotion.

One of the key challenges is understanding the different economic environments that exist in different countries. In some countries, prices may be lower due to lower labor or material costs, while in others, prices may be higher due to higher taxes or other factors. It's important for companies to be aware of these economic environments and to adjust their prices accordingly.

Another challenge is understanding the different cultural environments that exist in different countries. In some cultures, promotion may be seen as pushy or aggressive, while in others it may be seen as a sign of confidence. It's important for companies to be aware of these cultural environments and to adjust their promotion strategies accordingly.

Another important aspect of international pricing and promotion is currency exchange rates. The value of different currencies can fluctuate greatly, and it's important for companies to be aware of these fluctuations and to adjust their prices accordingly.

In conclusion, international pricing and promotion are important elements of any international business strategy. They help companies to reach new customers, increase revenue, and expand into new markets. However, there are a number of challenges that companies need to be aware of when it comes to international pricing and promotion. These include understanding the different economic environments that exist in different countries, understanding the different cultural environments that exist in different countries, and understanding the different currency exchange rates that exist in different countries. This chapter provides an overview of the key elements of international pricing and promotion, highlighting the importance of understanding and adapting to different economic, cultural and currency environments in different countries.

VIII

International Product Development

International product development is the process of creating new products or modifying existing products for international markets. It involves a number of different steps, including market research, product design, testing, and launch. The success of international product development depends on a company's ability to identify and understand the needs and preferences of its target market, as well as its ability to adapt its products to meet those needs.

One of the key steps in international product development is market research. This involves gathering information about the target market, including information about consumer needs, preferences, and buying habits. Market research can also include information about the competitive environment, as well as information about the legal and regulatory environment in the target market.

Once the market research has been completed, the next step is product design. This involves creating the product itself, including its features, packaging, and branding. It's important for companies to consider the cultural and regulatory environment of the target market when designing their products. For example, certain colors or symbols may have different meanings in different cultures, and products may need to meet different safety and environmental regulations in different countries.

Once the product has been designed, it's important to test it to ensure that it meets the needs of the target market. This can include focus groups, beta testing, and other forms of market testing.

Finally, once the product has been developed and tested, it can be launched into the target market. This includes everything from packaging and branding to distribution and promotion.

In conclusion, international product development is a critical process for any company looking to expand into international markets. It involves a number of different steps, including market research, product design, testing, and launch. Successful international product development depends on a company's ability to identify and understand the needs and preferences of its target market, as well as its ability to adapt its products to meet those needs. This chapter provides an overview of the key elements of international product development, highlighting the importance of market research, cultural and regulatory environment consideration, testing, and launch in the process of creating successful international products.

IX

International Business Models

When expanding into international markets, companies must decide on the best business model to use. There are several international business models that companies can choose from, including exporting, licensing, franchising, and wholly-owned subsidiaries. Each model has its own advantages and disadvantages, and the choice of which model to use will depend on the company's goals, resources, and the specific characteristics of the target market.

Exporting is the most common form of international business, and it involves selling products or services to customers in other countries. The advantages of exporting include low start-up costs and the ability to test the market before making a larger investment. However, exporting also has its drawbacks, such as the need to navigate tariffs and import regulations, and the potential for language and cultural barriers.

Licensing involves giving a foreign company the right to use a company's intellectual property, such as patents or trademarks, in exchange for a fee or royalties. This can be a good way to enter a new market without a large investment, but it also means giving up control over the brand and intellectual property.

Franchising is similar to licensing, but it also involves the transfer of business processes and management systems. This can be a good way to enter a new market quickly and with a proven business model, but it also requires a significant investment.

Wholly-owned subsidiaries involve setting up a new business entity in a foreign country and controlling it directly. This can be a good way to enter a new market with a large investment and the ability to control the brand and business processes, but it also involves a significant amount of risk and resources.

Lastly, Joint venture model, is when two or more companies form a new entity to achieve a common goal. It can be a good way to enter a new market with the help of a local partner and also to share the risks and costs.

In conclusion, each international business model has its own set of advantages and disadvantages, and the choice of which model to use will depend on the company's goals, resources, and the specific characteristics of the target market. It is important for companies to carefully evaluate their options and choose the model that best fits their specific needs.

X

Foreign Direct Investment and Mergers and Acquisitions

In today's globalized economy, foreign direct investment (FDI) and mergers and acquisitions (M&A) are two of the most important strategies for international business development. FDI involves a company investing in a foreign country, either by establishing a new business or by acquiring an existing business. M&A involves the purchase of one company by another, either through a merger or an acquisition.

FDI and M&A are attractive strategies for international business development because they allow companies to expand their operations into new markets, access new resources, and gain access to new technologies. FDI also allows companies to benefit from the lower costs of production in foreign countries, while M&A can provide access to new products, services, and markets.

FDI and M&A can be risky strategies, however, as they involve significant financial and legal risks. Companies must be aware of the laws and regulations of the countries in which they are investing, as well as the potential political and economic risks associated with foreign investments. Companies must also be aware of the potential for cultural differences between the countries in which they are investing and the countries in which they are operating.

In order to successfully implement FDI and M&A strategies, companies must have a clear understanding of the markets in which they are investing, the potential risks associated with the investments, and the potential benefits of the investments. Companies must also have a clear understanding of the legal and regulatory requirements of the countries in which they are investing, as well as the potential cultural differences between the countries in which they are investing and the countries in which they are operating.

FDI and M&A can be powerful tools for international business development, but they must be used with caution. Companies must carefully consider the potential risks and rewards of their investments, and must be aware of the legal and regulatory requirements of the countries in which they are investing. With careful planning and consideration, FDI and M&A can be effective strategies for expanding a business globally and increasing profitability, while also providing opportunities for innovation and diversification.

౭౦

XI

International Strategic Alliances and Joint Ventures

In today's globalized economy, international strategic alliances and joint ventures are becoming increasingly important for businesses looking to expand their operations and increase their market share. Strategic alliances and joint ventures allow companies to leverage the resources, expertise, and networks of their partners to gain access to new markets, technologies, and customers.

These partnerships can take many forms, from simple agreements to share resources and knowledge to more complex joint ventures that involve the sharing of ownership and profits. Regardless of the structure, the goal of these alliances is to create a mutually beneficial relationship that allows both parties to benefit from the collaboration.

The benefits of international strategic alliances and joint ventures are numerous. Companies can gain access to new markets, technologies, and customers, while also reducing costs and risks associated with international expansion. Additionally, these partnerships can help companies build relationships with local partners, which can be invaluable in navigating the complexities of international business.

However, there are also risks associated with international strategic alliances and joint ventures. Companies must be aware of the potential for cultural differences, language barriers, and legal issues that can arise when working with partners from different countries. Additionally, companies must be aware of the potential for conflicts of interest and the need to protect their intellectual property.

Despite the risks, international strategic alliances and joint ventures can be a powerful tool for businesses looking to expand their operations and increase their market share. By leveraging the resources, expertise, and networks of their partners, companies can gain access to new markets, technologies, and customers, while also reducing costs and risks associated with international expansion. With careful planning and consideration, these partnerships can be a powerful tool for businesses looking to grow and succeed in the global economy.

XII

International Trade and Tariffs

In today's global economy, international trade and tariffs are essential components of international business development. Tariffs are taxes imposed on imported goods, and they can be used to protect domestic industries from foreign competition. Tariffs can also be used to raise revenue for governments, or to protect certain industries from foreign competition.

International trade is the exchange of goods and services between countries. It is an important part of global economic growth, as it allows countries to specialize in certain industries and to benefit from the comparative advantages of different countries. International trade also helps to reduce poverty and inequality, as it allows countries to access goods and services that they may not be able to produce domestically.

Tariffs can have both positive and negative effects on international trade. On the one hand, tariffs can protect domestic industries from foreign competition, allowing them to remain competitive in the global market. On the other hand, tariffs can also raise the cost of imported goods, making them less attractive to consumers. This can lead to a decrease in international trade, as countries may be less likely to purchase goods from abroad.

In order to ensure that international trade is beneficial to all countries involved, governments must carefully consider the effects of tariffs on international trade. Tariffs should be used to protect domestic industries, but they should also be used in a way that does not impede the flow of goods and services between countries. Governments should also consider the effects of tariffs on the global economy, as tariffs can have a significant impact on global economic growth.

International trade and tariffs are essential components of international business development. By carefully considering the effects of tariffs on international trade, governments can ensure that international trade is beneficial to all countries involved. This will help to promote global economic growth and reduce poverty and inequality.

XIII

International Business and Government Relations

In today's globalized world, international business and government relations are essential for successful international business development. Governments play a key role in providing the necessary infrastructure and resources for businesses to operate and grow. They also provide a platform for businesses to interact with other countries and to access new markets.

Government relations are a critical component of international business development. Governments can provide access to resources, such as capital, technology, and labor, that are essential for businesses to succeed. They can also provide access to markets, which can be beneficial for businesses looking to expand their operations. Additionally, governments can provide incentives and regulations that can help businesses to remain competitive in the global market.

Government relations can also be beneficial for businesses in terms of risk management. Governments can provide protection from political and economic risks, such as currency fluctuations, trade restrictions, and other external factors. Governments can also provide access to legal and regulatory frameworks that can help businesses to remain compliant with local laws and regulations.

Finally, government relations can be beneficial for businesses in terms of public relations. Governments can provide access to public relations tools, such as media outlets, that can help businesses to build their brand and reputation. Governments can also provide access to public relations experts who can help businesses to craft effective messages and campaigns.

In conclusion, government relations are an essential component of international business development. Governments can provide access to resources, markets, risk management, and public relations tools that can help businesses to succeed in the global market. By leveraging government relations, businesses can gain a competitive edge and achieve long-term success.

XIV

International Business and Legal Issues

In today's globalized economy, international business and legal issues are becoming increasingly important for companies looking to expand their operations. As businesses expand into new markets, they must be aware of the legal and regulatory frameworks in place in each country. This chapter will explore the various legal and regulatory issues that must be considered when conducting international business, as well as strategies for navigating these complexities.

When conducting business abroad, companies must be aware of the various laws and regulations that govern international trade. These laws can vary significantly from country to country, and it is important to understand the implications of each. Companies must also be aware of the various international treaties and agreements that may affect their operations. Additionally, companies must be aware of the various cultural and social norms that may impact their business dealings.

In addition to the legal and regulatory issues, companies must also consider the various financial and economic issues that may arise when conducting international business. Companies must be aware of the various exchange rates and currency fluctuations that may affect their operations. Additionally, companies must be aware of the various taxes and tariffs that may be imposed on their products and services.

Finally, companies must also consider the various ethical and social issues that may arise when conducting international business. Companies must be aware of the various labor laws and regulations that may be in place in each country, as well as the various environmental regulations that may be applicable. Additionally, companies must be aware of the various cultural and social norms that may impact their operations.

By understanding the various legal, financial, economic, ethical, and social issues that may arise when conducting international business, companies can develop effective strategies for navigating these complexities. Companies must be aware of the various laws and regulations that may be applicable in each country, as well as the various international treaties and agreements that may affect their operations. Additionally, companies must be aware of the various financial and economic issues that may arise, as well as the various ethical and social issues that may be applicable. By taking all of these factors into consideration, companies can minimize potential risks and maximize potential rewards in their international business endeavors. It is also important for companies to maintain transparency and open communication with stakeholders and local communities, as well as to respect and adhere to local cultures and customs. By considering all of these factors, companies can develop strategies that are not only legally and financially sound, but also socially and ethically responsible.

XV

International Business and Ethics

In today's globalized world, international business and ethics are inextricably linked. As businesses expand their operations across borders, they must consider the ethical implications of their decisions. Companies must be aware of the cultural, legal, and economic differences between countries and strive to ensure that their operations are conducted in a manner that is respectful of local laws and customs.

At the same time, businesses must also be mindful of the ethical implications of their actions. This includes ensuring that their operations are conducted in a manner that is consistent with the values and principles of the company. Companies must also be aware of the potential for unethical practices, such as bribery and corruption, and take steps to prevent them.

In addition, businesses must be aware of the potential for conflicts of interest. This includes avoiding situations where the interests of the company conflict with the interests of its customers, suppliers, or other stakeholders. Companies must also be aware of the potential for conflicts of interest between different countries and strive to ensure that their operations are conducted in a manner that is respectful of the interests of all parties involved.

Finally, businesses must be aware of the potential for environmental and social impacts of their operations. Companies must strive to ensure that their operations are conducted in a manner that is respectful of the environment and the communities in which they operate. This includes taking steps to reduce their environmental footprint and to ensure that their operations are conducted in a manner that is respectful of the rights of workers and other stakeholders.

In conclusion, international business and ethics are inextricably linked. Companies must be aware of the potential for ethical and legal issues, conflicts of interest, and environmental and social impacts of their operations. By taking steps to ensure that their operations are conducted in a manner that is respectful of local laws and customs, the interests of all stakeholders, and the environment, businesses can ensure that their operations are conducted in an ethical and responsible manner.

XVI

International Business and Social Responsibility

In today's globalized world, international business and social responsibility are inextricably linked. Companies must recognize their responsibility to the communities in which they operate, as well as the global environment. To ensure sustainable growth, businesses must take into account the social, economic, and environmental impacts of their operations.

The concept of corporate social responsibility (CSR) has become increasingly important in international business. CSR is a business approach that considers the ethical, social, and environmental implications of a company's operations. It involves taking into account the interests of stakeholders, such as employees, customers, suppliers, and the local community, when making decisions.

Businesses must also consider the impact of their operations on the environment. Companies must strive to reduce their carbon footprint and minimize their environmental impact. This can be achieved through the use of renewable energy sources, reducing waste, and investing in green technologies.

In addition, businesses must ensure that their operations are compliant with international labor standards. This includes providing safe working conditions, fair wages, and the right to collective bargaining. Companies must also ensure that their supply chains are free from forced labor and child labor.

Finally, businesses must recognize their responsibility to the communities in which they operate. This includes investing in local infrastructure, providing job opportunities, and supporting local charities and initiatives.

In conclusion, international business and social responsibility are essential for sustainable growth. Companies must take into account the interests of stakeholders, reduce their environmental impact, ensure compliance with international labor standards, and invest in the local community. By doing so, businesses can ensure that their operations are socially responsible and contribute to global growth.

XVII

International Business in Emerging Markets

In today's globalized world, international business and social responsibility are inextricably linked. Companies must recognize their responsibility to the communities in which they operate, as well as the global environment. To ensure sustainable growth, businesses must take into account the social, economic, and environmental impacts of their operations.

The concept of corporate social responsibility (CSR) has become increasingly important in international business. CSR is a business approach that considers the ethical, social, and environmental implications of a company's operations. It involves taking into account the interests of stakeholders, such as employees, customers, suppliers, and the local community, when making decisions.

Businesses must also consider the impact of their operations on the environment. Companies must strive to reduce their carbon footprint and minimize their environmental impact. This can be achieved through the use of renewable energy sources, reducing waste, and investing in green technologies.

In addition, businesses must ensure that their operations are compliant with international labor standards. This includes providing safe working conditions, fair wages, and the right to collective bargaining. Companies must also ensure that their supply chains are free from forced labor and child labor.

Finally, businesses must recognize their responsibility to the communities in which they operate. This includes investing in local infrastructure, providing job opportunities, and supporting local charities and initiatives.

In conclusion, international business and social responsibility are essential for sustainable growth. Companies must take into account the interests of stakeholders, reduce their environmental impact, ensure compliance with international labor standards, and invest in the local community. By doing so, businesses can ensure that their operations are socially responsible and contribute to global growth.

XVIII

International Business in Developed Markets

In today's globalized economy, international business in developed markets is a key factor in the success of any business. Companies must be able to identify and capitalize on opportunities in these markets in order to remain competitive and grow.

When entering a developed market, businesses must be aware of the local regulations and laws that govern the market. It is important to understand the cultural and economic differences between the home country and the target market. Companies must also be aware of the competitive landscape and the potential for success in the market.

Businesses must also consider the cost of doing business in

the target market. This includes the cost of labor, materials, and other resources. Companies must also consider the cost of marketing and advertising in the target market. Additionally, businesses must consider the cost of transportation and logistics when entering a developed market.

In order to succeed in a developed market, businesses must have a clear strategy for growth. This includes identifying potential customers, understanding the competitive landscape, and developing a marketing plan. Companies must also be aware of the potential risks associated with entering a developed market.

Finally, businesses must be aware of the potential for success in the target market. Companies must be able to identify and capitalize on opportunities in the market in order to remain competitive and grow.

International business in developed markets is a complex and challenging endeavor. Companies must be aware of the local regulations and laws, the cost of doing business, and the potential risks associated with entering a developed market. Additionally, businesses must have a clear strategy for growth and be able to identify and capitalize on opportunities in the market in order to remain competitive and achieve success. With the right strategy and approach, businesses can capitalize on the potential for growth in developed markets and achieve success in the global economy.

XIX

International Business in BRIC Countries

In the past two decades, the BRIC countries – Brazil, Russia, India, and China – have become increasingly important players in the global economy. As a result, international businesses have had to adjust their strategies to take advantage of the opportunities presented by these countries.

The BRIC countries offer a unique set of advantages for international businesses. For example, Brazil has a large and growing consumer market, while Russia has a wealth of natural resources. India has a highly educated workforce and a rapidly growing technology sector, and China has a large and growing manufacturing base.

At the same time, the BRIC countries also present a number

of challenges for international businesses. For example, Brazil and Russia have complex regulatory environments, while India and China have a history of protectionism. Additionally, the BRIC countries have different cultural norms and business practices, which can make it difficult for international businesses to operate in these countries.

Despite these challenges, international businesses have been able to successfully navigate the BRIC countries and take advantage of the opportunities they present. For example, many international businesses have established joint ventures with local companies in the BRIC countries, allowing them to access local markets and resources. Additionally, international businesses have been able to leverage the BRIC countries' growing consumer markets and technology sectors to expand their operations.

In conclusion, the BRIC countries present a unique set of opportunities and challenges for international businesses. By understanding the local markets and regulations, and by leveraging the advantages of the BRIC countries, international businesses can successfully expand their operations and take advantage of the opportunities presented by these countries.

XX

International Business in Africa

In recent years, Africa has become an increasingly attractive destination for international businesses looking to expand their operations. With a population of over 1.2 billion people, the continent offers a vast and diverse market for companies to explore.

The African continent is home to a wide range of natural resources, including oil, gas, minerals, and agricultural products. This makes it an ideal location for businesses looking to capitalize on these resources. Additionally, the continent is home to a number of rapidly growing economies, such as Nigeria, Kenya, and South Africa, which offer a wealth of opportunities for businesses to explore.

The African continent is also home to a number of unique cultural and political environments, which can present both challenges and opportunities for international businesses. Companies must be aware of the local customs and regulations in order to ensure their operations are compliant with local laws. Additionally, businesses must be prepared to navigate the complex political and economic landscape of the continent.

Despite the challenges, there are a number of advantages to doing business in Africa. The continent offers a wide range of investment opportunities, with a number of countries offering attractive incentives for foreign investors. Additionally, the continent is home to a number of rapidly growing markets, which can provide businesses with a wealth of potential customers.

In order to succeed in the African market, businesses must be prepared to invest in the local infrastructure and workforce. Companies must also be willing to work with local partners in order to ensure their operations are compliant with local laws and regulations. Additionally, businesses must be prepared to adapt their strategies to the unique cultural and political environments of the continent.

By taking the time to understand the African market and its unique challenges, international businesses can capitalize on the continent's vast potential. With the right strategies and investments, businesses can take advantage of the continent's natural resources, rapidly growing economies, and diverse customer base. With the right approach, international businesses can find success in the African market.

୧୬

XXI

International Business in Middle East

In the Middle East, international business is a rapidly growing sector. With its strategic location, abundant resources, and a large, diverse population, the region is becoming an increasingly attractive destination for global businesses.

The Middle East is home to some of the world's most dynamic economies, with a range of opportunities for international businesses. The region is rich in natural resources, including oil and gas, and has a well-developed infrastructure. It also has a large, educated workforce, making it an ideal location for businesses looking to expand their operations.

The Middle East is also a hub for international trade, with

many countries in the region having strong trading relationships with other countries around the world. This makes it an ideal place for businesses to establish a presence and take advantage of the region's many opportunities.

The Middle East is also home to a number of international organizations, such as the World Trade Organization, the Arab League, and the Organization of Islamic Cooperation. These organizations provide a platform for businesses to engage in international trade and investment.

The Middle East is also a major destination for foreign direct investment. With its strong economic growth, the region is becoming increasingly attractive to foreign investors. This is due to its low cost of doing business, its strong legal and regulatory framework, and its access to a large, educated workforce.

The Middle East is an ideal location for businesses looking to expand their operations and take advantage of the region's many opportunities. With its strategic location, abundant resources, and a large, educated workforce, the region is becoming an increasingly attractive destination for global businesses. With its strong economic growth, the region is becoming increasingly attractive to foreign investors, making it an ideal place for businesses to establish a presence and take advantage of the region's many opportunities.

XXII

International Business in Asia

In the ever-evolving global economy, Asia has become a major player in international business. With its vast population, diverse cultures, and rapidly developing economies, the region has become a hub for international business development.

From the bustling cities of Tokyo and Shanghai to the rural villages of India and Indonesia, Asia is home to a wide variety of cultures and industries. Businesses in the region have access to a wide range of resources, including a large and growing consumer base, a highly skilled workforce, and a wide range of natural resources.

The region is also home to some of the world's most advanced technology and infrastructure, making it an ideal location for businesses looking to expand their operations. Additionally, the region's governments have taken steps to create a more business-friendly environment, making it easier for businesses to operate in the region.

The growth of international business in Asia has been driven by a number of factors, including the increasing demand for goods and services from the region, the availability of resources, and the increasing number of businesses looking to expand their operations.

The region has also seen an increase in foreign direct investment, as businesses from around the world have sought to take advantage of the region's resources and potential. This has led to an increase in the number of multinational corporations operating in the region, as well as an increase in the number of joint ventures and strategic alliances between businesses from different countries.

The growth of international business in Asia has also been driven by the region's increasing economic integration. As countries in the region become more interconnected, businesses have been able to take advantage of the region's resources and potential. This has led to an increase in the number of businesses operating in the region, as well as an increase in the number of joint ventures and strategic alliances between businesses from different countries.

The growth of international business in Asia has been a major factor in the region's economic development. As businesses from around the world have sought to tap into the vast market potential of Asia, many have turned to foreign direct investment (FDI) and mergers and acquisitions (M&A) as key strategies for entering the market. This has led to a significant increase in cross-border investment flows and the establishment of new business operations in the region.

However, while FDI and M&A can be powerful tools for international business development, they must be used with caution. Companies must carefully consider the potential risks and rewards of their investments, and must be aware of the legal and regulatory requirements of the countries in which they are investing. With careful planning and consideration, FDI and M&A can be effective strategies for expanding a business globally and increasing profitability, while also providing opportunities for innovation and diversification.

Additionally, as the economic and political conditions in Asia are constantly changing, companies must be aware of the various legal, financial, economic, ethical, and social issues that may arise when conducting international business in the region, and develop effective strategies for navigating these complexities.

XXIII

International Business in Europe

In the modern world, Europe is a major hub for international business. With its diverse cultures, languages, and economies, Europe is a prime destination for businesses looking to expand their operations. From the United Kingdom to Germany, France to Italy, and beyond, Europe offers a wealth of opportunities for businesses to grow and thrive.

The European Union (EU) is a major factor in the success of international business in Europe. The EU provides a single market for goods and services, allowing businesses to operate freely across the continent. This has led to increased competition, which has in turn driven down prices and improved quality. Additionally, the EU has implemented a number of regulations to ensure fair competition and protect consumers.

In addition to the EU, there are a number of other factors that make Europe an attractive destination for international business. The continent is home to some of the world's most advanced economies, with strong infrastructure and a highly educated workforce. This provides businesses with access to a wide range of resources and expertise. Furthermore, Europe is home to a number of international organizations, such as the World Trade Organization, which provide businesses with access to global markets.

For businesses looking to expand into Europe, there are a number of strategies that can be employed. One of the most important is to develop a comprehensive understanding of the local market. This includes researching the local culture, language, and regulations, as well as understanding the competitive landscape. Additionally, businesses should consider forming strategic partnerships with local companies, as this can provide access to resources and expertise. Finally, businesses should consider investing in marketing and advertising to ensure their products and services are well known in the local market.

Overall, Europe is an attractive destination for international business. With its diverse cultures, languages, and economies, Europe provides businesses with a wealth of opportunities for growth and success. By understanding the local market, forming strategic partnerships, and investing in marketing and advertising, businesses can take advantage of these opportunities and expand their operations in Europe.

One key advantage for companies doing business in Europe

is access to the world's largest single market, the European Union (EU). The EU's single market allows for the free movement of goods, services, capital, and people within its member states, providing businesses with a large potential customer base and a streamlined regulatory environment. Additionally, Europe is known for its highly educated and skilled workforce, providing a pool of talented employees for companies to draw from.

However, while doing business in Europe can be very rewarding, it is important to note that it also comes with its own set of challenges. Companies must be familiar with the various laws and regulations that may be applicable in each country, as well as the various international treaties and agreements that may affect their operations. Additionally, companies must be aware of the various cultural, linguistic, and economic differences that exist across Europe, and adapt their strategies accordingly.

Overall, while Europe is an attractive destination for international business, it requires careful planning and consideration to navigate the complexities of the different cultures, languages, economies, laws and regulations that are unique to each country.

XXIV

International Business in America

In the modern world, international business in America is a rapidly growing field. With the rise of globalization, companies are increasingly looking to expand their operations into new markets. This has led to a surge in the number of international businesses operating in the United States.

The United States is a prime destination for international businesses due to its strong economy, large consumer base, and well-developed infrastructure. Companies can benefit from the country's vast resources, including its highly skilled workforce, advanced technology, and access to global markets. Additionally, the United States offers a variety of incentives for international businesses, such as tax breaks, grants, and other forms of financial assistance.

For international businesses looking to establish a presence in the United States, there are a few key considerations. First, they must understand the local laws and regulations that govern their operations. This includes understanding the tax code, labor laws, and other legal requirements. Additionally, businesses must be aware of the cultural differences between the United States and their home country. This includes understanding the language, customs, and values of the local population.

In order to succeed in the United States, international businesses must also develop a comprehensive strategy for growth. This includes identifying potential markets, developing a marketing plan, and creating a competitive advantage. Additionally, businesses must be prepared to invest in research and development, as well as in the training and development of their employees.

Finally, international businesses must be prepared to adapt to the ever-changing landscape of the United States. This includes staying up-to-date on the latest trends in technology, consumer behavior, and the global economy. By doing so, businesses can ensure that they remain competitive and successful in the United States.

International business in America is a rapidly growing field, and companies that are able to successfully navigate the complexities of the US market can reap the rewards of a successful venture. By understanding the local laws and regulations, developing a comprehensive growth strategy, and staying up-to-date on the latest industry trends and technology, businesses can thrive in the American market.

The United States is home to one of the world's largest and most diverse economies, with a wide range of industries and sectors to choose from. It is also a leading destination for foreign direct investment, making it an ideal location for companies looking to expand globally. Additionally, America's legal system and market-oriented economy provide a stable and predictable business environment.

However, doing business in the US can also be challenging. The country's complex legal system and regulatory environment can be difficult to navigate, and businesses must be aware of the various laws and regulations that apply to their operations. Companies also need to be aware of the cultural and linguistic differences that exist in different regions of the US, and adapt their strategies accordingly.

Overall, while America is a highly attractive destination for international business, companies must be prepared to navigate the complexities and challenges that come with doing business in such a large and diverse market. With careful planning, market research, and a strong strategy, businesses can successfully expand and thrive in America.

XXV

International Business and Digitalization

In the digital age, international business has become increasingly interconnected and complex. As technology advances, businesses must adapt to the changing landscape of global markets and develop strategies to remain competitive. Digitalization has enabled businesses to expand their reach and access new markets, while also providing opportunities to streamline operations and reduce costs.

The digital revolution has opened up a world of possibilities for international business. Companies can now access global markets with ease, allowing them to reach new customers and expand their customer base. Digitalization has also enabled businesses to reduce costs by automating processes and eliminating the need for manual labor.

Additionally, digitalization has enabled businesses to access data and insights from around the world, allowing them to make informed decisions and stay ahead of the competition.

In order to capitalize on the opportunities presented by digitalization, businesses must develop a comprehensive strategy for international business development. This strategy should include an analysis of the global market, an understanding of the competitive landscape, and a plan for leveraging digital technologies to gain a competitive advantage. Additionally, businesses must ensure that their digital infrastructure is secure and compliant with international regulations.

Finally, businesses must be prepared to adapt to the ever-changing digital landscape. As technology advances, businesses must stay ahead of the curve and develop strategies to remain competitive. By leveraging digitalization to gain a competitive advantage, businesses can ensure their success in the global market.

In conclusion, digitalization has revolutionized international business, providing businesses with unprecedented opportunities to expand their reach and access new markets. By developing a comprehensive strategy for international business development, businesses can leverage digital technologies to gain a competitive advantage and ensure their success in the global market.

OTHER BOOKS OF THE AUTHOR

1. The Moments When I Met God
2. Kashiyile Theertha Pathangal
3. GURU GYAN VANI
4. Abhiprerak Gita
5. ASSI SE JAIN GHAT TAK
6. Hopelessness of Arjuna
7. The Soul and It's True Nature
8. Sense of Action (Karma)
9. Action through Wisdom
10. Action through Wisdom
11. THEORY AND PRACTICAL OF EVERY ACTION
12. LOGICAL UNDERSTANDING OF THE SUPREME
13. THE IMPERISHABLE SUPREME
14. Yatra Nishadraj se Hanuman Ghat Tak
15. Yatra Karnatak Ghat se Raja Ghat Tak
16. Yatra Pandey Ghat se Prayagraj Ghat Tak
17. Yatra Ranjendra Prasad Ghat se Dattatreya Ghat Tak
18. YaatraSindhiya Ghat se Gwaliar Ghat Tak
19. Yatra Mangala Gauri Ghat se Hanuman Gadhi Ghat Tak
20. Yatra Gaay Ghat Se Nishad Ghat Tak
21. MAA GANGA, GHATEN EVM UTSAV
22. Ganga Arti Dev Deepavali evam Any Utsav
23. Potentials of Digitalized India
24. VEDIC CONSCIOUSNESS
25. A Brief Introduction to Vedic Science
26. Kashi ke Barah Jyotirling
27. IMPACT OF MOTIVATION
28. Let's have a Milky Way Journey
29. Color Therapy in a Nutshell

30. Rigveda in a Nutshell
31. Yajurveda in a Nutshell
32. Samveda in a Nutshell
33. Atharva Veda in a Nutshell
34. Ayushman Bhava - Ayurveda
35. Srimad Bhagavad Gita and Upanishad Connection
36. Srimad Bhagavad Gita - an attempt to summarize each chapter.
37. Facts and Impact of Nakshatra
38. Astro Gems - NAVARATNA
39. Ekadashi - A Concise Overview
40. A Concise View of Hanuman Chalisa
41. Inspirational Gita
42. Nakshatraranyam
43. Summary of 18 Mahapuranas
44. Synopsis of 18 Upa Puranas
45. Rigvediya Upanishads
46. Shukla Yajurvediya Upanishads
47. Krishna Yajurvediya Upanishads
48. Samavediya Upanishads
49. Atharvavediya Upanishads
50. The Seven Great Sages
51. From Rocket Scientist to President Dr. APJ Abdul Kalam
52. The Visionary's Voice - Quotes of Dr. APJ Abdul Kalam
53. The Wisdom of Swami Vivekananda: Insights and Inspiration from a Legendary Spiritual Teacher
54. Ayurvedic Remedies from the Garden
55. Sages and Seers
56. Rising Strong – Motivational Stories of Women
57. Beyond Flames -Mystery stories of Funeral Ghat Manikarnika
58. The Origins of Tulsi: A Look at the Mythological Roots of the Plant"

CONTACT

DR. JAGADEESH PILLAI

MBA & PhD in Vedic Science

Four Times Guinness World Record Holder

Winner of Mahatma Gandhi Vishwa Shanti Puraskar and
Global Peace Ambassador

Gemology, Astro & Vastu Consultant - Spiritual Counselor

Consultant for designing World Record Ideas

Efficient Tarot Card Reader

9839093003

myrichindia@gmail.com

drjagadeeshpillai@facebook

drjagadeeshpillai@instagram
jagadeeshpillai@youtube

www. JAGADEESHPILLAI.com

৪৩

|| LOKAHA SAMASTHAHA SUKHINO BHAVANTU ||

ॐ

CPSIA information can be obtained
at www.ICGtesting.com
Printed in the USA
BVHW030806140623
665884BV00008B/793